MYSTERY at FAIRLY FIELD

by Judy Nayer
illustrated by Marisol Sarrazin

Modern Curriculum Press
Parsippany, New Jersey

Computer Colorizations by Jacki Hasko

Cover and book design by Denise Ingrassia

Modern Curriculum Press
An imprint of Pearson Learning
299 Jefferson Road, P.O. Box 480
Parsippany, NJ 07054–0480

www.pearsonlearning.com

1-800-321-3106

ISBN 0-7652-1372-9

2 3 4 5 6 7 8 9 10 UP 08 07 06 05 04 03 02 01 00

**Modern
Curriculum
Press**

Contents

To Matthew, my favorite Little Leaguer

Chapter 1
Time for Baseball!

It was Saturday. Lisa Hira woke up early. She could see that it was a beautiful day. "Yes!" she said. Lisa hurried to get dressed. Today was the first baseball practice for the Falcons.

Lisa rushed down the stairs and into the kitchen. She ate breakfast. Then she picked up her new baseball mitt. She punched her hand into the glove.

"I'm ready," she said to her dad. "Bye, Mom," she called as she left.

Mr. Hira and Lisa went to the car. They saw a moving van pull into the driveway next door.

"Who's moving in?" asked Lisa.

"Oh," said Mr. Hira, "I heard from Mr. Grant that Mrs. Grant's father is moving in with them."

Mr. Hira drove down B Street. Katy
Stone was waiting for them at the end of
the block.

"Coach Barnes called this morning,"
Katy said to Lisa in the car. "Some of our
equipment is missing."

"Oh, no," Lisa said.

Chapter 2
Bad News

Lisa and Katy joined Andy Lopez and Zack Gibson at the baseball field. They started to tell the boys about the equipment. Then the coach started talking.

"Some of you have heard that I have bad news," Coach Barnes said. "One of our equipment bags is missing. It was there when the coaches got the equipment ready. The bag had our bats in it, so we won't hit today. We'll practice throwing and catching."

10

The team split up into groups. Lisa, Katy, Andy, and Zack made a square. They practiced throwing the ball as if they were at the bases.

"I wonder what happened to the equipment bag," said Katy.

"I do, too," said Zack. "Do you think someone took it?"

"Maybe," said Andy. "How are we going to play without bats?"

"I don't know," said Lisa. "I think the B Street Kids have a mystery to solve!"

Chapter 3
A New Neighbor

After practice, Katy, Lisa, Zack, and Andy helped Coach Barnes. They looked through the equipment room. The bat bags that belonged to the other teams were there. None of the bags said Falcons on it.

They heard a horn honk. "That's my
dad," said Lisa. She and Katy ran for the
car.

At home, the girls practiced in Lisa's
backyard. Katy threw the ball. It went right
over Lisa's head and into the Grants' yard.

Someone threw the ball back over the hedge. "Is that your ball?" said a man.

"Yes, thanks," said Lisa. "You must be Mrs. Grant's father."

"That's right," said the man. "I'm Mr. Smith. I just moved here from Los Angeles. Do you like baseball?" he asked.

"Yes!" said Lisa. "Today was our first team practice."

"We didn't get to bat today because our bats are missing," said Katy.

"That's too bad," said Mr. Smith. "May I come to a game?" he asked.

"Sure!" said the girls.

Chapter 4
Good News

The next Saturday, Lisa went to practice again. This time Coach Barnes had some good news.

"It seems that the Fairly Falcons have a friend," he told everyone. "Someone dropped off a bag full of new bats. There is a box of new team shirts, too."

Lisa picked out a shirt that looked like her size. "Lucky number 7," she said as she put it on. Then she found a note in the box. "Listen!" she said. "It says, 'Have a great baseball season!'"

"That's it?" asked Zack.

"Didn't anyone sign it?" asked Andy.

"Who do you think it's from?" asked Katy.

"I don't know," said Lisa. "The only name on the box is the company that makes the equipment. Now we have another mystery to solve!"

Practice that day did not go well for Lisa. She couldn't get a hit. "What happened to lucky number 7?" she wondered.

Coach Barnes asked Lisa to get the team list after practice. "I left it on the table in the office," he said.

Lisa put her bat down. She ran to the office. She picked up the list and turned to go. Then she tripped over something.

Lisa looked down to see what she had tripped over. It was an old bat bag! Lisa picked it up. She saw the name Falcons printed on the cloth. She also saw a big hole in the bottom. Where were the bats?

Chapter 5

Game One

The next Saturday was the day of the first game! The Falcons were playing the Eagles. Lisa was worried about striking out. She was also thinking about the empty bat bag.

At the ball field, Coach Barnes called
everyone over. He told them where they
would be playing. Katy was at first base.
Zack was at second base. Andy was
pitching. Lisa would be playing between
second and third base as the shortstop.

The Eagles were batting first. The
Falcons took the field. The first half of the
inning went well. Lisa threw the ball to
Katy for the first out. Then Andy struck
out the next two players.

It was the Falcons turn to bat. Katy was the first batter. She hit the ball hard and ran all the way to second base.

Then it was Lisa's turn to bat. The pitcher threw the ball. Lisa swung at it. "Strike!" called the umpire.

Lisa missed two more times. "Strike three!" called the umpire. Lisa walked sadly back to the bench.

When the Eagles came up to bat again, Lisa was sitting on the bench. The first Eagle walked to home plate. Lisa saw a mark on his bat. It looked like an F instead of an E.

She turned to Rick D., who played first base. "Rick," Lisa said, "does that look like a letter F on that bat?"

Rick looked. "Yes, it does," he said. "Tell Coach Barnes after the game."

The rest of the game did not go well. Lisa struck out every time she came up to bat. The Falcons lost 6 to 4.

"Don't worry," said Coach Barnes. "We'll win the next one."

Lisa told Coach Barnes about the Eagles' bat. "Let's go ask their coach about it," he said.

The Eagles' coach opened her team's bat bag. She pulled out the bats.

"You're right," she said. "The bats marked with an F must be your bats. How did they get in our bag?"

Chapter 6

Help From a Friend

When Lisa got home, Mr. Smith was outside. "You look like you have lost your best friend," he said to Lisa.

"Well," said Lisa, "that's how I feel. I just struck out at our first game."

"Even big league players strike out," Mr. Smith said.

"Maybe," said Lisa, "but they don't strike out every time."

"It was just the first game," said Mr. Smith. "You'll have a great baseball season!"

"Thanks," said Lisa. Then she thought, "Where have I heard that before?"

The next day was Sunday. Lisa wanted to practice batting. She and her dad went to the park. They saw Mr. Smith there with his grandson.

Mr. Smith said to Mr. Hira, "Do you mind if I pitch a few balls to Lisa?"

"Sure," Mr. Hira said.

Lisa was puzzled. Mr. Smith didn't look like a ballplayer. Yet he sounded as if he knew what he was doing. He pitched the ball. Lisa swung. She missed.

"You know what, Lisa?" said Mr. Smith.
"You were watching me, not the ball. Keep
your eye on the ball."

Lisa tried. It was hard not to look at Mr.
Smith or the bat. Then she swung. She
heard a crack. She had hit the ball!

"That's it, Lisa!" called Mr. Smith.

"That's it?" asked Lisa. "That's all I have to do?"

"That's a lot of it," said Mr. Smith. "Practice watching the ball all the way to the bat. Also remember not to swing too high or too low."

Lisa hit a few more. She was so happy.
"That's great, Lisa!" said Mr. Hira. "I
guess we owe Mr. Smith a big thanks."
"We sure do!" said Lisa.

Lisa went over to Andy's house when she got home. She told him about Mr. Smith.

"Maybe he played baseball when he was young," Andy said.

"Maybe," said Lisa. Then she jumped up. "I have an idea," she said.

Chapter 7
Game Two

Lisa and Katy were warming up at Fairly Field for the second game. Rick D. came up to them. "If it isn't No-Hit Hira," he teased.

Lisa's face got red. She didn't let Rick's words bother her. Today, Number 7 was feeling lucky.

The Falcons were playing the Bears. Lisa was first to bat. She watched the pitch. It was too high. Lisa didn't swing.

"Ball!" cried the umpire.

The next pitch came. Crack! The ball flew over the shortstop's head. Lisa raced to first base. She was safe! Then she looked up. Mr. Smith was cheering from the bleachers!

    In the sixth inning the score was tied 8 to 8. There were runners on first and second base. Lisa was up at bat again. She swung hard at the first pitch. Crack! The ball went high in the air. Lisa ran to first. Then she ran to second base and to third base.

The second-base player threw the ball to third base. The ball flew over the third-base player's head. Lisa ran as hard as she could to home plate.

"Safe!" called the umpire.

40

Chapter 8
The Mystery Is Solved

The final score was Falcons 11, Bears 8.
The whole team crowded around Lisa.
"Way to go!" Rick D. cheered.

"Where did you learn to hit like that?" Andy and Zack asked Lisa.

"My neighbor, Mr. Smith, has been helping me," said Lisa. She pointed to Mr. Smith.

Each team began to pick up their equipment. Lisa saw a little boy helping the Bears' coach.

"Who is that?" Lisa asked Katy.

"That's Coach Gomez's little boy, Jimmy," Katy said.

"Was Jimmy with Coach Gomez the day the coaches sorted the equipment?" Lisa asked Coach Barnes.

"Yes," he said.

"I think I know what happened to our bats," Lisa said.

"I was right," Lisa told the others later. "Jimmy was helping the coaches. Our bats fell out because there was a hole in the bag. Jimmy doesn't know the letters E or F, so he put the bats in the Eagles' bag. He put our bag under the table in the office."

Just then Mr. Hira came over. "You were right about something else, too," he said to Lisa. "You asked me to call the company that sent the new bats and shirts. They were ordered by Mr. Willie Smith on B Street."

Coach Barnes looked up. "Willie Smith!" he said. "There was a Willie Smith who was a big league ball player in the 1960s. He played for the Los Angeles Angels. If he is the same man, it would be great if he could help out our team."

"I am the same man. I'd be happy to help," Mr. Smith said.

With Mr. Smith's help, the Falcons played the best they had ever played. It was a great baseball season.

Glossary

base   [bays] a bag on the ground that baseball players run to

bleachers   [BLEE churz] long benches that are seats for people to sit on to watch a game

coach   [kohch] a person who teaches or trains others

company   [KUM puh nee] a business; a group of people who work together

equipment   [ih KWIHP munt] the special things needed to play a game or do an activity

league   [leeg] groups joined together for a reason, such as a sport

pitching   [pihch ing] throwing a baseball to a batter

umpire   [UM pyr] a person who rules on how a baseball game is played